Who's the Goose That Lays the Golden Eggs?

An Essay on Political Economy

———————— ∾ ————————

By Leon Johnson

* James Carville coined the phrase "It's the economy, stupid!" during Bill Clinton's 1992 presidential campaign against George H. W. Bush in order to emphasize the vital role a healthy economy plays in the lives of every citizen.

Editorial work and production management by Eschler Editing.
Cover design by Jason Robinson.
Interior print design and layout Ben Welch.
eBook design and layout by Eugene Woodbury.

Published by Scrivener Books

First Edition: November 2017

Printed in the United States of America

10 9 8 7 6 5 4 3 2

ISBN 978-0-9986254-6-1

Acknowledgments

My deepest gratitude to all my family and friends who supported me in the writing of this book. It truly takes a village to create a book. Thanks to the team at Eschler Editing, including Heidi Brockbank, Anna Allen, and Michele Preisendorf for their dedication, as well as Jason Robinson of Atlas Graphics for making my cover suggestions a reality, and Ben Welch for his excellent work on the book design.

To workers and consumers everywhere.
You are the true wealth creators.
We are indebted to you.

Foreword

WE ARE all consumers. Spending money is what drives the economy. These statements are so transparently obvious that most people don't stop to really think about them. They are so obvious that they are taken for granted. In doing so, the obvious implications are often overlooked. People don't think about consumers living in an interdependent regime. They don't think about how poverty affects the entire economy. They don't consider that people who suffer poverty are not capable of spending enough to sustain the economy. Businesses depend on consumer spending, and workers depend on businesses for their jobs. People don't realize that when workers don't get a living wage, their bosses are essentially starving the entire economy. Those groups who want to repeal social security, and who want to deport undocumented immigrants, don't think about the giant hole this would leave in the economy. Global warming deniers don't think about the cost of global warming to their businesses.

I have written this book for the purpose of bringing attention to these concerns and encourage people to consider their ramifications. I cannot sit idly by and let people ignore the potential consequences. Our survival depends on our thinking about them. My survival, your survival, everyone's survival. We're all in the same boat.

I used to hear people say that the government should not kill the goose that lays the golden eggs. The people who said this were the chief executive officers (CEOs) of big corporations. What they were saying was that they didn't want government to overtax businesses because it would reduce their profit, which was the source of their prosperity.

So what's with "the goose that lays the golden eggs"? The saying refers to an old fable that goes like this: There once was a peasant who went shopping at the local marketplace. The peasant bought a goose, and, to his delight, it turned out that this goose laid eggs made of gold. Accordingly, the peasant became rich. One day the peasant became hungry, and he killed the goose and cooked it. The peasant had a great dinner, but he lost the golden eggs and his wealth along with them.

This story can be applied to our current society. We can ask ourselves, "Who's the goose laying the golden eggs?" Is it the corporations? According to venture capitalist and entrepreneur Rick Hanauer, it's not the corporations but the consumers. He says consumers are the country's true job creators. Corporations have been growing ever more wealthy, but not one cent of that money has created jobs. He himself has created and invested in dozens of manufacturing, retail, medical, and Internet companies, but he gives the credit to consumers.[1]

Consumers are potentially the most powerful group in America. They can bring the most powerful corporation to its knees simply by not patronizing it.

Investment counselor A. Gary Shilling says that if you want to understand economics, you should pay attention to the consumers.[2] Some CEOs are undermining their own profits by waging war against the consumer. It is the consumer who is the goose laying the golden eggs, and corporate extremists are the peasant killing the goose. With that said, though, I do not wish to belittle the accomplishments of the entrepreneurs. It takes ambition, intelligence, ingenuity, and courage to start a business. And it is worth noting that our entrepreneurs have accomplished much. But they have not eliminated poverty.

I want to make my position completely understood: yes, corporations have advanced our economy through entrepreneurship, but they have done this because consumers have bought their products and services. They have not brought an end to poverty, and poverty is a drain on their profits. I do not approve of a command economy because such a thing stifles entrepreneurship. I believe in free enterprise for everyone, not just for the elite—for labor as well as management—because we are all consumers. I believe the role of government is to promote justice and to provide protection, both economically and politically, against internal and external threats. This requires some degree of regulation but not total control. I feel it's essential to leave entrepreneurs free to compete. I believe in freedom under law, but I also believe that the laws need to be just. Call me "liberal" or "conservative"—I am both, but I prefer to be called "progressive."

Who are the consumers? They are working men and women, and many of them are being paid minimum wage or close to it. The minimum wage was originally meant to be a living wage. But it has not kept up with inflation and has become a poverty wage. Persons on poverty wages have to round out their living with welfare, which is barely enough for survival. Congress has let working men and women down.

Welfare was originally meant to support single moms, because mothering is also a job. But corporate extremists don't think so. They believe single moms on welfare are "takers," not "givers."

What an insult.

If single moms are doing their job well, they are raising good workers who have good work habits. Corporate extremists also say a woman's place is in the home and that women should not work outside the home. But apparently single moms don't count.

Now, I'm not in favor of getting something for nothing. I believe in a solid work ethic. But how do corporate extremists and others define "solid work ethic"? They say, "Make a profit, and you automatically do a service." But they have it backward. They should be saying: "Do a service, and you can receive a profit." There's a world of difference between the two.

Corporate extremists consider that anyone on welfare without a job is a "taker." They claim that in order to get the benefit of welfare, people should have to earn welfare by working.

Does anyone else see what's wrong with that? If people are working, they shouldn't need welfare. They do indeed earn it. The employer is the one who gets the welfare because the government is supplementing the workers' wages with the money the employer should be paying them. So who's the taker in this situation?

They tell the indigent, "If you want to better your life, get a job." But the fact is that most indigents already have jobs. Who are these indigents? They are such people as the retail clerks in chain stores like Walmart, fast-food workers, dishwashers, customer-assistance representatives, home health-care aides, factory workers, and farm laborers. In 2013, there were about 46 million Americans living in families with an income less than the poverty line—$11,702 for individuals and $23,021 for a family of four.

There were also those whose income was above the poverty line but who still couldn't afford basic needs, such as food, clothing, health care, housing, transportation, and childcare. If you include these individuals among the indigent, there were more than 146 million additional working-class indigents. If a crisis occurred, such as sickness or an accident, they were all in serious trouble. Meanwhile, companies like Walmart, McDonald's, Pizza Hut, and Target were making big bucks. The workers of these companies made on average about $13,900, while their CEOs received $9.4 million. Shareholders were awarded $175 billion in dividends.[3] So who, I ask, were the takers in this situation?

The country has been going through the most serious economic crisis to have hit the nation since the Great Depression. This crisis was caused by big banks acting like riverboat gamblers with the people's money. The result was the subprime mortgage crisis that began in 1998. Between 1998 and 2006, low-income families lost somewhere between $71 billion and $83 billion in asset values because of subprime loans.

Nobody noticed. Nobody cared.

Then in 2006, the number of low-income housing foreclosures dramatically rose. In 2013, former chairman of the Federal Reserve Paul Volcker, among others, warned the administration that if it did not rein in the banks, something terrible would happen.

It did.

In 2008, the crisis hit the middle class. Now everyone noticed. The subprime mortgage crisis sent the entire world economy plummeting.[4]

By 2013, there was some improvement as the housing market recovered. Sales were up 29 percent compared with the year before.[5] Car sales have also been increasing since then. Car sales made up only 4 percent of the gross national product but were responsible for half of the economic growth in the first quarter of 2013. Consumers were buying cars before interest rates went up in order to keep their monthly payments low. The housing market helped as well because contractors, plumbers, and electricians were buying pickups.[6] Consumer confidence rose, and the stock market rallied.[7] Standard and Poor's 555-stock index doubled. In addition, 135,000 new jobs were added to the economy.[8] American households now had a cumulative net worth of $70 trillion, and people had extra money to spend.[9]

But we were not out of the woods yet. People were reluctant to spend that extra money. Before the crisis, they'd spent five cents of every dollar on housing and stocks. Now they were spending barely half that sum. In addition, people were less willing to take the risks that got them into this mess in the first place; they were more cautious about borrowing for housing and for buying stocks.[10] And not everyone had extra money to spend. For instance, 24 percent of Americans said they had trouble putting food on the table the year before, while in 2007, it was only 16 percent.[11] More than three-quarters of Americans were living from paycheck to paycheck, with barely enough money for an emergency.[12] The number of children living in poverty rose to 23 percent in 2011, while in 2005, it was only 19 percent.[13] Many households had not recovered from their losses of the last six years. House prices were still 22 percent less than they were before the crisis,[14] and today more than 7.3 million mortgage holders are still underwater.

The housing recovery is a mirage anyway. About the only ones who can buy houses are investors who can afford to make all-cash payments and who outbid every other buyer. They are the ones cashing in on this bonanza, not those who have already bought homes and are waiting to see when, or whether, their homes will recover their original value. Not those who are burdened with mortgages. Not first-time buyers. And those who lost their homes should forget about ever owning a home again.[14] And those who lost well-paying jobs may as well forget about getting them back. Automation will take them.[15]

About 49 percent of work activities can now be turned over to automation. About 59 percent of CEOs plan to reduce their workforce due to automation during the next five years. Only 26 percent will hire new employees for the same reason. Nearly 15 percent of 130 million jobs can be mostly or completely automated. Hamburger flippers can be robots. Machines can take food orders as well as persons. Shelf stockers can be replaced by robots.[16]

The butcher, the baker, the candlestick maker—all are threatened by automation. And if you are in a profession, don't think you are safe. More than seventy professions can be as much as 90 percent automated. Data processing done by robots? About one in five financial and insurance companies do it. Even ophthalmology lab technicians can be replaced. Ah, but journalists are safe, you say. Robots can't write stories, right? Wrong! A software suite called "Wordsmith" writes dozens of stories every month about sports and financial accounts.[17]

In 2013, individual citizens were not the only ones in trouble. The city of Detroit was filing for bankruptcy. It couldn't pay the $18 billion it owed to retirement funds, unions, and a host of private creditors. And Detroit is not a small town but one of our major metropolises. According to Michigan governor Rick Snyder, the problem was six decades in the making. People were going to be in trouble. What to do? The *Detroit News* said they "may as well call a hearse as an ambulance." Many other municipalities, such as Oakland, Chicago, and Philadelphia were sinking into the same hole. The *Wall Street Journal* asked, "If Detroit isn't too big to fail, is any city?"[18]

That was 2013. There was a recovery in 2014, but it was a "Goldilocks recovery": not too hot, not too cold, but not just right.[19] There was something for the optimist and something for the pessimist. In 2014, the unemployment rate was down to a record low of 5.1 percent. The stock market was booming. But don't toss confetti or pop the champagne cork yet. Wages were still low. The $533,657 of the middle-income scale adjusted for inflation was 6.5 percent lower in 2014 than it was in 2007 and 7.2 percent lower than in 1999, and there was no evidence of a reversal. And it was true for every age and racial group.[20] If you told these people we were in a recovery, they wouldn't believe you.

The economy has improved since then. But again, don't celebrate yet. At the time this essay was published, this recovery was still in the Goldilocks stage. Yes, average wages are rising, unemployment is decreasing, and the stock market is booming. So what's wrong with the economy? Here's what's wrong. Over the last three decades, the median wages of white-blue collar workers—defined as the 68 percent without a college degree—has fallen by 10 percent. And their plight is more than financial. The mortality rate of blue-color workers between the ages of forty-five and fifty-four has risen by 22 percent since 1999 due to alcohol, drug abuse, and suicide.[21] Rustbelt streets are lined with boarded-up stores and pawn shops, and the countryside is dotted with derelict factories and empty warehouses. Since 1979, millions of jobs have been lost, and factories have closed forever.

Knowing the background of this situation and understanding its seriousness, you may ask yourself, "What's being done about all this?" The president has been funneling money back into the economy to replace the money the banks lost by gambling it away. This money has been spent on programs to raise people out of poverty, to save homes, and to create jobs.

The Federal Reserve has been doing the same by buying securities each month. This is called "quantitative easing" (QE), and its purpose is to lower interest rates and boost markets and, in the process, strengthen the economy.

Neither Obama's spending nor the Federal Reserve's quantitative easing have been enough. These economic stimuli have helped, but we have not crossed the Jordan River. We have not reached the promised land of full recovery. What can be done? What more?! What else?!

Some may suggest we cut taxes. Some wonder, "Wouldn't this stimulate growth by keeping more money in the pockets of the consumer?" But this idea has been tried, and it didn't work. Former president George W. Bush got tax cuts passed on a massive scale, and his administration saw the slowest economic growth since World War II. Former presidents George H. W. Bush and Bill Clinton got taxes raised, and we had a boom economy. Not only that, but an analysis by the Congressional Research Service concluded that since World War II, there has been no correlation between tax cuts and economic growth.[22]

Some say government stimulus is the wrong approach. They say that the nation is in economic trouble, so the government should economize and cut back on spending and make budget cuts. This makes sense—for individuals. This is austerity. But wait a minute! When a country is experiencing hard times, isn't it already experiencing austerity? The way to restore the economy is to spend. Spending drives the economy. After all, that's what the economy is about—spending.[23]

Some budget cuts are not fair. Low-income people are dependent on safety-net programs, and cutting those programs is unfair because those who can least afford to sacrifice are sacrificing, while those who can afford to sacrifice aren't. Budget cuts simply do not make economic sense. They reduce buying power; low-income people are consumers too. In fact, some budget cuts are dangerous.

Take the case of our infrastructure. Bridges and overpasses are collapsing because they haven't been kept in repair. In Skagit, Washington, for instance, a 160-foot section of a bridge collapsed when a truck bumped into one of the bridge's steel trusses, sending several cars twenty-five feet off the bridge into ice-cold water. People could have been killed but, fortunately, were not. A few days later, an overpass crumbled, injuring seven. America's bridges have an average life span of forty-two years before they need to be repaired or replaced. The Federal Highway Administration says that $90 billion would be needed to do that. The highways are sixty years old, and the railroads are older than that.[24] According to the American Society of Civil Engineers (ASCE), decaying roads, railways, bridges, and transit systems are costing $129 billion, the cost of operating vehicles is $97 billion, and various delays are costing $32 billion. And costs would increase exponentially. Within ten years, businesses would pay $430 billion, household incomes would fall $7,000, and exports would fall $28 billion.[25]

But Congress is not in a spending mood. Congress rejected President Obama's request for $50 billion to repair roads and bridges, saying the request was "an unfunded wish list." Presently, Congress could borrow at a bargain rate of 1 percent interest before the interest rate got bigger.[26]

Not only do our bridges and roads need fixing, so does our justice system. In every state, the public-defender system is underfunded. Lawyers frequently must handle as many as four- to five-hundred cases a year. Often, the first time they meet their clients is in court, and they don't have time to do enough research for the case. The result is often a miscarriage of justice. For example, one man spent twenty-four years in prison based solely on the testimony of a single witness. The man's lawyer didn't get around to mentioning that the witness was mentally ill and had a history of hallucinations.[27]

Columnist E. J. Dionne says that the deficit is not the real problem. Deep cuts have slowed growth. At the time this was printed, the deficit was reduced from 10 percent in 2009 to 4 percent in 2013, but there were still 11.3 million people out of work.[28]

The International Monetary Fund—that champion of fiscal responsibility—advised the United States to loosen up on its budget cuts because they cut the nation's economic growth by almost half. They said that budget cuts were not only harmful but also unnecessary.[29]

Now it's important to mention here that I'm not advocating irresponsible borrowing. (And neither is the International Monetary Fund.) That's how we got into this mess. But should we economize at the expense of safety? Should we economize at the expense of justice? Those who demand budget cuts claim to be conservative. But do they know what it means to be conservative? They don't have a clue. Conservatives may act responsibly, but these cuts are irresponsible. How many people buy houses and cars with cash down? Only the wealthy can do that. Business enterprises must borrow in order to get established, and the banks profit from this. And bonds are nothing more than IOUs that help businesses to get established. This is responsible borrowing.[30]

What can we do? What else is there? No one has come up with any other solution. Some economists have simply given up. Paul Volker, former secretary of the US Department of the Treasury, reported to the annual research conference of the International Monetary Fund that the depressed economy of the United States has become the norm. In other words, we can forget about hoping that things will ever get better. We have tried everything.[31]

Or have we? There is one obvious detail, an important item in the economy, that economists have consistently overlooked. They seem to have a blind spot. I have never read or heard of any economist giving this blind spot so much as a mention. College graduates with PhDs have never been educated on the condition of the poor because they have never been poor. The thing they have failed to see is the thing that has the most pervasive effect on the lives of the working poor—the minimum wage.

A simple solution to our economic problem would be to raise the minimum wage to a living standard. Opponents of raising the minimum wage claim that most minimum-wage earners are teens who are supported by their parents and are just looking for extra cash for nonessentials. Research by the Economic Policy Institute, however, has found otherwise. The institute has found that the average age of minimum-wage earners is thirty-five, not seventeen; that 88 percent are over twenty; and that more than a third are over forty. Furthermore, the research has revealed that more than one in four has children. Also, 44 percent of these individuals work full-time. These minimum-wage earners are neither part-time teen dependents nor high school drop-outs. In fact, only 29 percent lack a high-school degree, and more than 40 percent have a college education.[32]

"But," you say, "wages are an expense. If the minimum wage were raised, wouldn't that bankrupt small businesses? Workers would lose their jobs."

When you say that, you are saying that workers have to live in poverty in order to keep their jobs. "But wouldn't raising the minimum wage cause inflation?" you continue. "If the boss has to pay extra cash for increased wages, wouldn't he have to raise prices to cover the expense?" When you say that, though, you are saying that workers must live in poverty to keep inflation down. When you say these kinds of things, you are saying that our economic system doesn't work. Is that what you mean? Give me a break!

I understand the problem facing small businesses. They are not yet doing as well as they were before the recession, and the reason is this: people are not spending money like they used to. And one reason people aren't spending money is that too many people are only getting the minimum wage, or close to it. If the boss pays his workers more money, what will the workers do with the money? They will spend it, of course. This will create profit. This will create jobs. Will it create inflation? If one company raises its prices, but another company does not, which company will consumers patronize? It's called competition. With all that extra money in circulation, who will need to raise prices? The boss will get his money back in trade. It will be an economic stimulus, once a month, all year long. And it will not be a loan the government will have to pay back. It will get people off welfare, which will be a savings for the national budget. Not only that, but it will also painlessly raise taxes. If people are making more money, they can pay more taxes. There would be no excuse for budget cuts of essential services, and there would still be enough to pay off the national debt.

On the other hand, if the boss keeps more money for himself at the expense of his workers, he would have more money, right?

Wrong. Not in the long run.

The workers would have less money to spend. This would lead to recession, and profits would be reduced. Workers would have to go on welfare. This would mean more taxes, and profits would be further reduced. Low wages and low profits would mean less money to tax, reducing the national treasury, forcing it to make painful budget cuts that would curtail necessary services. This, in fact, is what has happened. The 68 million working but still poor represent millions of dollars in profits lost, as well as a loss of revenue.

The bottom line is this: when the bosses starve the workers, they are also starving the economy. This is not only an economic issue; it is also a moral issue. If the boss expects his workers to do an honest day's work for an honest day's pay, the workers have a right to expect an honest day's pay for an honest day's work. It's the Golden Rule. "But wouldn't a law mandating a living wage be an infringement on our freedom?" you ask. Whose freedom? And freedom for what? Freedom for some to commit injustice against others? A poverty wage is an injustice. Everyone knows this. The purpose of government is to dispense justice, not dispense *with* justice. A living-wage law is an essential responsibility of government.

At the dawn of the twentieth century, Henry Ford invented the assembly line, which lowered the price of the cars his company was making. He also paid his employees a good wage so that they could afford to buy the cars they were making. Henry Ford was so successful that other companies followed his example and paid their employees good wages. The economy prospered.[33] But this was not maintained. Two of the factors responsible for the declining economy were continuous inflation and some people being on a fixed income. This resulted in a roller-coaster economy of boom and bust. Recessions are as much a matter of underconsumption as they are of overproduction.

Here's what happened: As prices rose, more and more low-income people were pushed over the poverty cliff. Less money was spent by consumers, and recession was inevitable. As prosperity returned, prices rose again, and the vicious circle kept repeating itself. But when prosperity did return, people on a fixed income were left behind, resulting in a two-level economy. This caused stagflation—the upper level pushed prices up while the lower level dragged commerce down.

According to the White House Council, the minimum wage was intended to be a living wage. But it has not kept up with inflation. As a result, labor's share of the national wealth has been reduced. According to the White House Council of Economic Advisers, in 1947, labor's share of nonfarm profit was 65 percent. In 2013, it plummeted to 57 percent. This represents a displacement of $750 billion annually from labor to capital.[34]

Neither has it kept up with labor's increasing productivity. According to the Heritage Foundation, labor's productivity increased 100 percent over the last forty years, but its wages increased only 77 percent.[35] As *Washington Post* columnist Robert J. Samuelson notes, "Labor's shrinking share curbs consumer spending. . . . A well-functioning economy is a circular process by which one person's spending becomes another person's income, which is then spent again."[36] In other words, the economy works like a circulatory system. Money flows around the economy like blood flowing through the heart, arteries, and veins. If the boss pays his workers starvation wages, the money circulation is clogged, like hardening of the arteries.

The Kellogg Foundation and Jobs for the Future conducted public-opinion surveys that found most Americans agree that the minimum wage should be increased. But in the past, come election time, they forgot about that. They thought only of their own self-interest. Prolabor candidates were afraid to make an issue of it. They were afraid of losing votes because the public failed to speak out. America turned its back on working men and women, and now we are suffering a prolonged recession.

But now people are starting to talk about it. For example, in the wake of a disappointing 2013 Black Friday, columnist Daniel Gross said on DailyBeast. com that if retailers want "a boom in holiday sales," they should "loosen the purse strings" and pay their workers a decent wage.[37] Another columnist, Eugene Robinson of the *Washington Post*, agreed that the working poor need to earn more money.[38] Most economists, as well as most citizens of both parties, believe the minimum wage should be raised.[39] But then, the citizens were already ahead of the economists.

Not only that, but they were doing something about it. Several burger chains, including In-N-Out in California, paid their workers $10.50 an hour, with medical benefits, paid vacations, and a 401(k) plan, giving the lie to the assertion that fast-food restaurants are cheap food at a thin profit margin. This isn't true.

For example, McDonald's CEO Don Thomson made $13.8 million in 2012.[40]

Governments are acting too. In SeaTac, a suburb of Seattle, voters backed a $15 minimum-wage proposal. Legislators of California and Massachusetts also raised their minimum wage to over $10.[41] President Obama said he would support a federal minimum wage of $10.10.[42] A congressional bill, the Fair Minimum Wage Act of 2013, was proposed, raising the minimum wage to $10.19 over three stages. Both proposals would index the minimum wage to inflation, an important step in making it effective.[43] Rick Hanauer, business man and entrepreneur, believes that if the minimum wage were raised to $15, it would boost the economy by $45 billion. It would also counter the effect of lower-paying jobs replacing higher-paying jobs.[44]

According to a February 2014 Congressional Budget Office report, the $10.10 minimum wage President Obama proposed would raise nine hundred thousand people out of poverty and increase the income of 16.5 million low-wage workers. It would also cost up to five hundred thousand jobs.[45] Many people questioned this report. I was one of them. But after I had a conversation with my niece, I had second thoughts. She has a small business owner renter who has raised only enough for the payroll and occasionally doesn't have enough for the rent. My niece generously overlooked this, and she pointed out to me that a business with little or no profit margin could not afford to raise wages until conditions improved. Otherwise she was wholeheartedly in favor of raising the minimum wage. She agreed with me that the current minimum wage is an injustice. Companies that have little or no profit margin will need help.

Suppose we add $45 billion to the economy by raising the minimum wage; how should that extra money be used? One urgent need is repair of the nation's infrastructure. Congress was talking about it during the Obama administration. They were talking about long-term aviation funding but couldn't agree. The Federal Aviation Administration had been on a shutdown, costing $30 million per day in lost ticket sales-tax revenue. For surface transportation, House Republicans had a six-year plan for $35 billion per year. Transportation Committee chair John L. Mica (R Fla.) said that this could be leveraged to $675 billion by means of a public-private partnership. Another proposal for $109 billion had bipartisan support, but Mica said this would bankrupt the Federal Highway Trust Fund. All this may not matter because Republicans proposed that investments be slashed by one-third. Representative Nick J. Randal (D W. Va.) said that the ASCE report (which I have previously discussed) underscores the folly of trying to do more with less.[46]

Repairing the infrastructure will provide jobs. But more will need to be done. Currently, the government spends only 0.1 percent of its gross national product on helping workers deal with changes in the workplace. These "readjustment programs" deal with everything from military-base closings to the needs of Appalachian coal miners but include nothing for workers who've lost their jobs to automation.[47] With the additional $45 billion, it wouldn't be difficult to give workers a scholarship to attend a technological school to learn the skills necessary to keep up with the new technology.

Jobs lost to automation is a serious problem. But according to Joel Mokyr, economic historian at Northwest University, technological stagnation would be worse.[48] But if jobs don't keep pace with automation, the whole system will collapse because not many people will have enough money to buy the products and services produced by automated companies.

Uber developed a self-driving car they sent on a two-hundred-kilometer journey from Fort Collins to Colorado Springs, Colorado. Yes, self-driving vehicles still need drivers to monitor them.[49] Driverless cars are only good on sunny days and not in fog or snow, nor are they good in situations where human intelligence is needed.[50]

This is encouraging. Machines can never replace human intelligence. All that needs to be done is to retrain workers with new skills. There are 3.5 million high-skill jobs in specialized manufacturing waiting for them.[51] There are about 530,000 more computing jobs looking for workers, but only 60,000 students graduated in computer science in 2015.[52]

It would be helpful for government to support free community colleges that train workers for high tech skills. This would not only create more jobs, it would also create more opportunities for entrepreneurs. The federal government is already in the research business. NASA has created many inventions that are useful outside of space exploration. Here are a few:

- *Water filters*: These were originally intended to fulfill the need for clean water in space in extreme conditions for a longer period of time. Water filters have existed since the 1950s, but NASA's filters are treated with silver ions that neutralize pathogens in water.

- *Cordless tools*: In 1961, Black + Decker invented battery-powered tools. For the Apollo moon trip, they needed a lightweight drill strong enough to excavate samples of moon stuff. NASA partnered with Black + Decker to refine the technology and invented the battery-magnet drill. From this, we got medical tools, handheld vacuum cleaners, and much more.

- *Safety grooving*: NASA experimented with grooving airplane runways. This was then applied to highways.

- *Adjustable smoke detectors*: NASA needed one in Skylab, the first space station. They teamed with Honeywell.

- Long-distance communication: Before humans were sent into space, NASA invented and launched satellites that could communicate with earth. There are now two hundred communication satellites that use similar technology so we can communicate long-distance.[53]

The NASA bureaucracy is controlled by the government, not the scientists. Government goals are not always the same as scientific goals, so sometimes the bureaucracy stands in the way. This is counterproductive. Give the scientists more freedom, and they will give more in return.[54]

The main opponent of raising the minimum wage is the American Legislative Exchange Council (ALEC), an organization of CEOs and legislators founded by Paul Weyrich, Henry Hyde, Lou Barnet, and Mark Rhodes in 1973.[55] Members of ALEC are very religious—they worship the almighty dollar. They know the price of everything and the value of nothing. ALEC is supported by corporations who craft "model legislation" behind closed doors and ask lawmakers to sponsor it in the legislature. In return, lawmakers are given hefty bribes, dinners in plush hotels, and vacation trips they can't afford on their own income. ALEC even provides childcare so that the parents can have fun. If the state doesn't prohibit it, the lawmakers finance their trips to ALEC meetings with public funds—at the taxpayer's expense. If that isn't possible, ALEC covers the expense. The corporations get a tax break for their donations, which is also at the taxpayer's expense. In other words, legislators are working hand in glove with lobbyists and are getting big bucks for it.[56]

ALEC members will not bargain. They make no concessions. If they don't get their way, they obstruct no matter the consequences. This is hardly a democratic process. Corporations get something for this. The tobacco industry owes a lot to ALEC. As everyone knows, the tobacco industry sells poison. But people still buy their poison. What everyone is less aware of, however, is that ALEC also supports companies who poison the environment. But we'll talk about that later.

Right now, let's talk about ALEC's agenda. ALEC infringes on workers' rights. It tries to roll back civil-rights legislation, and it challenges restrictions on pollution. It opposes necessary government regulations, and it aims to privatize public services.[57] ALEC has gained control of the Republican Party. No, I'm not being partisan. Honest Republicans do not like what has happened to their party. Many have been booted out of the party. In the state legislature of Utah, my home state, several so-called Republicans are members of ALEC. Senator Curtis Bramble, Senator Wayne Niederhauser, and Representative Chris N. Herrod are all cochairs of ALEC. Governor Gary Herbert is an alumni.

I'm sure true Republicans would be as interested in exposing ALEC as Democrats are. Republicans as well as Democrats have been turning down chances to run for Congress. They don't think anything can be accomplished there. Ohio lieutenant governor Kim Reynolds, who turned down a chance to run for an open seat, said, "At the federal level, it's so partisan, it's dysfunctional."[58] But now there seems to be a sea of change in Congress. Since the 2012 election, Republican leaders have been making a devastating critique of their party's performance. The Republican National Committee published a one-hundred-page document, the "Growth and Opportunity Project."

It tells the Republican Party to "stop talking to itself." It describes many voters as seeing the GOP as "scary," "narrow minded," and "full of stuffy old men." It suggests it should build bridges to minorities, women, and the poor.[59] Of course, Tea Party members reject this report. There are two kinds of Republicans in Congress, and Congress is divided between them. In the Senate, John McCain, the moderate, and Ted Cruz, the Tea Party member, were calling each other "wacko bird."[60] The two groups have been unable to work together, and in the 2015 Congress, the House of Representatives was so divided and unmanageable that House Speaker John Boehner resigned in despair, and no one wanted to replace him.[61]

Democrats need to ally with honest Republicans to help them get their party back. Then Democrats could talk with someone who makes sense. Both parties are essential. Republicans demand personal responsibility, believing that individuals must take care of themselves. Democrats want community responsibility, believing that helping those who need help is in the public interest. We need both kinds of responsibility.

Of course, the two parties have differences of opinion. There are two kinds of differences. There are honest differences of opinion, and there are differences between right and wrong. The public needs to recognize the difference.

As I have said, ALEC wants to keep wages low. But I must be honest: ALEC isn't the cause of low wages—competition is. Competition is the friend of the consumer but the enemy of the worker. Businesses need to keep expenses low in order to compete. Wages are an expense. Even honest businessmen need to pare their wages in order to compete. But, more than that, they are generally opposed to any extra expense for whatever reason.

This includes safe and healthy working conditions. Moreover, they are opposed to any extra expense for the general good, including the safety and healthfulness of their products and conservation of the environment, even to save their own lives. That is why government regulation is necessary as part of our free-enterprise system. It is also the reason unions were organized. Yes, strikes often inconvenience consumers, and sometimes they inconvenience the economy as a whole, but the threat of strikes is the only way unions can achieve bargaining power, and when it comes right down to it, unions benefit the entire economy. They benefit workers, first of all, as consumers, which improves the entire economy because the economy depends on the consumer. Union workers are more likely to get fringe benefits. They get 18 to 28 percent more in health insurance, with 18 percent lower deductibles, and are more likely to receive these things after retirement. They also get 23 to 57 percent more in retirement and

26 percent more in vacation time. They also play a pivotal role in legislation on safety, health, overtime, and family medical leave. Union wages are 29 percent more than nonunion wages and 28 percent more if fringe benefits are included.[62]

I'm not saying unions are always right, but neither are their bosses. Unions and management need to cooperate for the sake of the economy. In some European nations, labor leaders are given a seat on the company board, a relationship called codetermination. This gives labor and management a chance to understand each other's points of view and prevent strikes.[63] This would be a good practice for America to adopt. Companies who trade with foreign nations are at an even greater disadvantage when they compete with cheap foreign labor.

I do not approve of free-trade treaties. Many jobs depend on tariffs for protection. It is generally agreed that NAFTA has had mixed results. Its purpose was to create jobs by promoting trade between Canada, Mexico, and the United States. Mexico was "to import products, not people." Trade has grown from $290 billion in 1993 to $1.1 trillion in 2016. It has increased employment for 14 million persons in jobs like retail, finance, and agriculture, and provided cheaper goods for consumers. About five million jobs depend on trade with Mexico, nine million jobs on trade with Canada.

On the other hand, nearly seven hundred thousand jobs were lost, mostly in manufacturing, and the wages of those who kept their jobs flatlined. Moreover, the trade balance between the United States and Mexico flip-flopped from a surplus of $1.7 billion to a deficit of $49.2 billion. And NAFTA didn't curb the flow of undocumented immigrants from Mexico, which increased from three million in 1994 to twelve million in 2007. Although Mexico gained about six hundred thousand jobs in manufacturing, it lost at least two million jobs in agriculture due to the import of corn and other produce from the United States. That is the reason for the increase of undocumented immigrants to the United States.[64]

A plan that results in pockets of poverty is not good, no matter how much overall improvement. A better way to improve the economy is to raise income, like wages and social security, and by implementing training for new skills.

But the other extreme—protectionism—would be just as bad. Small businesses depend on foreign trade. President Trump's proposed 20 percent border tax would seriously impact retail and manufacturing, who import much of their goods. It would not only create additional subsidies and inhibit job creation, but would also drive up prices, not only of small business but also on big ticket items like cars, electronics and appliances. According to the National Retail

Association, the average family would pay $1,700 per year on higher prices for goods.[65]

Advocates of free trade say that tariffs impede trade and prevent competition, which has the virtue of promoting excellence. I can't argue with that. Extreme protectionism is bad for trade. An export-based economy is a pirate economy. It takes money from other nations without giving money back. If every nation practiced this economy, it would create a situation like the widespread protectionism practiced during the Great Depression, which only made matters worse. For a sustainable economy, in international as well as domestic, money has to circulate.

One might think that if we changed to free trade, we would increase trade dramatically and open the door to competition, in which everyone would work hard to do better than everyone else. But in practical terms, the transition would create economic chaos because industries protected by tariffs would be in deep trouble. Anyway, not every nation would do this, so we would be giving the advantage to foreign imports. Besides, tariffs do not impede internal competition.

Under the pressure of competition to reduce costs, corporations export jobs by hiring cheap foreign labor. Americans lose jobs, and foreign workers are abused. American consumers can do something about this. They can boycott products made by these companies. They can shame the companies so that no one else will want to buy from companies with such bad reputations. Governments can play a role in this, by favoring states that guarantee a living wage for their workers and sanctioning states that don't. This is a better way to achieve prosperity than with free-trade treaties. Companies would make more profit by trading with well-paid consumers than they would by exploiting cheap labor.

I do not wish to make out the bosses as the bad guys. I recognize that competition is an irresistible force.

One way the United States can restore the economy is to repeal welfare. It is a waste of money the nation can't afford. I'm talking about corporate welfare—welfare for the wealthy. Big oil gets $37.5 billion from the government. By contrast, project-based tenants get $8.7 billion, and housing gets $6.6 billion. This has helped 4.5 million families.

Big pharmacy gets $270 billion. They buy up all the patents developed by tax-funded research, get a corner on the market, and jack up prices. Bernie Sanders is sponsoring a bill that would allow the government to buy up the patents and sell the drugs at cost.

Big agriculture gets $18 billion, originally meant to help farmers recover from the dust bowl of the 1930s. The median income of commercial farmers was $84,649 in 2011, which was 70 percent more than NASA's budget.

Big banks get $83 billion. The Federal Reserve allows them to borrow at lower interest rates than other banks. If they had to borrow at the same rate as other banks, the savings would be enough to double the budget for highways ($48.6 billion), Head Start ($10.1 billion), the Environmental Protection Agency ($7.89 billion), nutritional assistance for women, infants, and children ($6.2 billion), the National Park Service ($3 billion), and the Federal Deposit Insurance Corporation, with $5 billion left over.

Export-Import Bank gets $112 billion, of which multinationals get most. Of that, only ten companies get more than any other company. The top two hundred companies got $880 billion in federal contracts. Between 2007 and 2012, they spent $5.8 billion lobbying Congress, giving them an unfair advantage of over 30 billion more than is paid to the fifty million families on Social Security.

Those are subsidies. But there's more. There are tax cuts.

CEOs can write off inflated compensation packages due to a twenty-year-old law that allows them to do that. This is the amount the National Science Foundation funded for eleven thousand research projects and twenty-six Nobel laureates.

Top executives can write off their corporate jets, expensive cars, and chauffeurs as security, costing the taxpayer $300 million. This is half the entire budget of the Consumer Financial Protection Agency.

Capital gains is the money one makes when selling off investments. It is taxed at a lower rate (20 percent) than wages (35 percent). This amounts to $51 billion lost to the government. Only 53 percent of the population owns stocks. Of those who do, only 5 percent own two-thirds of it. If capital gains were taxed at the same rate as wages, 75 percent would come from the richest 0.3 percent.[66]

State and local tax incentives are supposed to attract businesses into the state and create jobs. This is done at the expense of the taxpayers—the consumers. This would be fine if it worked, but the problem is, it doesn't. Robert G. Lynch, author of *Do State and Local Tax Incentives Work*, discusses the conclusions of hundreds of research projects conducted on the issue. Two methods of research were used in the studies. In the interview method, business leaders were asked about what factors induced them to locate to a particular place. In the statistical method, several mathematical techniques were used to determine whether tax incentives influenced their decisions. The answer was a unanimous "no."[67]

Lynch describes that these "incentives" are actually disincentives. Companies who don't get the incentives are disadvantaged, so they cut back on production and hiring, and governments must either raise taxes or cut services to pay for the "incentives." He continues to say that the incentives are often given for political reasons that involve bribery, payoffs, and illegal campaign contributions. The incentives don't guarantee that companies will stay in the state. High-tech industries need to be located in the vicinity of universities or research centers, and other companies will locate according to a boss's personal preferences.[68]

Do State and Local Tax Incentives Work is no longer published because, sadly, no one has used it and no one is doing anything about it now. But the book can be checked out from the local library. It needs to be published again. It is a valuable weapon against corruption.

The total cost of all these handouts is $980.4 billion. Temporary Assistance to Needy Families ($17.3 billion), food stamps (7.3 billion) and earned income tax credit ($67.2 billion) combined, amounts to only one-tenth of this.[69]

Can you see the hand of ALEC in this? Corporate welfare benefits corporations at the expense of everyone else. ALEC claims to be conservative. But corporate welfare is not conservative. It is irresponsible. It is immature. If you want to be conservative, dump corporate welfare.

I do not object to giving a company a tax break or a subsidy if it gives something back. For example, I would be in favor of making small companies totally tax free if it would help them raise their wages, and if necessary, giving them additional subsidies or giving tax breaks to companies that do research and development.

What about that other welfare program, the one for the other end of the economic spectrum? Has it made loafers of us? "If we get something for nothing, why work for it?" you ask. Do you believe this? David Cay Johnston, author of *Perfectly Legal*, doesn't believe it. Congress lets business owners, investors, and landlords play by one set of rules filled with opportunities to hide income, fabricate deductions, and lower taxes, whereas wage earners operate under another, much harsher, set of rules in which every dollar of income from a job, a savings account, or stock dividend is reported to the government and taxes are withheld from each paycheck to make sure wage earners pay in full.[70]

This double standard reflects indifference and ignorance as well as greed. Tax policy is boring and complex, and most people don't know or care much about it. As this same author describes, our federal tax laws are often voted on without any public hearing, without any disclosure of who introduced this or that provision. Members of Congress routinely vote on tax bills they have never read, much less understood, even on a superficial level.[71] So tax policy is boring. Get over it!

Has our welfare system been a success? Has it reduced poverty? Yes, by 4 percent. That's not much. And it has cost $16 trillion on hundreds of programs. Should it be cut? Should it be repealed? But wait a minute—Johnson's War on Poverty, his famous antipoverty program has achieved some significant victories: reduced infant mortality, established health clinics in rural areas, improved once-neglected schools, raised college completion rates, and provided homes for the needy and put food in their mouths.[72]

That's not all. It has kept the economy going. People on welfare are consumers too. For example, food stamps subsidize stores as well as the people who use them; they get money they would not otherwise have. But still, welfare is expensive—much too expensive. True, it puts money back into the economy, but it does so by cannibalizing the economy. It should not be used as a steady income but only for emergencies. If you want to reduce welfare, there is a simple solution: raise the minimum wage to a living standard.

A significant group of consumers is people on Social Security. They are funded by a tax constantly being paid by the next generation of retirees, and they have earned it by paying it when they were working. Now they are funneling it back into the economy to the amount of more than $1 trillion a year.[73]

ALEC wants to repeal Social Security.

Think of what would happen to the economy if that were to happen! Think of what would happen to society! Think of what would happen to the legislators who would do such a stupid thing!

The population is growing because the Baby Boomer population is growing up. We will need more tax money to pay for Social Security and Medicare. Where are we going to get this money? Robert Samuelson thinks we will have to raise taxes. He says the candidates of both parties are unrealistic. The Republican candidates say they will cut taxes to stimulate the economy. The nonpartisan Tax Foundation says these tax cuts will cause a loss of tax revenues between $1.5 trillion and $10 trillion over a decade, and even by the most optimistic assumptions, the government could not absorb such losses. The Democratic candidates say they will raise the taxes of the super-rich. But even if these taxes were raised from 39.6 percent to 50 percent, they would only raise $100 billion in annual tax revenues, which is hardly enough to make Social Security and Medicaid sustainable. Samuelson says that sooner or later, we will have to raise taxes.[74]

There is a painless way to raise taxes: get more taxpayers. Raise the minimum wage to a living standard and it will create more taxpayers. It's the magic money tree the candidates are looking for. Let's hope they find it.

Discrimination is costly to consumers. People with talent are denied opportunity. Persons with less ability are given work for which they are less capable. The result is mediocrity.[75] For businesses, it results in lower productivity, bad publicity, court costs, and the cost of replacing workers who quit because of discrimination.[76] And there is the cost to the victims.

We have made progress since the days of discrimination in the early twentieth century. We have done away with the practice of "separate but equal." We have passed laws against discrimination. African Americans can live anywhere they want. They can shop anywhere they want. They can get any kind of job they want. They have come a long way. Right?

Well, discrimination has been largely eliminated, but prejudice is alive and well. Police are racial profiling. Even successful African Americans are experiencing hostility both in the workplace and out of it. And there is still discrimination within the workplace. Integration has not worked well for African Americans. On average, African American incomes are 60 percent lower than that of whites, and whites live six to seven years longer.[77]

The costs are not only material. There are emotional costs. William James, a late-nineteenth-century psychologist, pointed out that there is no greater punishment than marginalization and social isolation.

It results in feelings of impotent despair. "Impotent despair"—what does that mean? One cannot know unless one feels it oneself. White people have accused African Americans of being too sensitive, of being paranoid. But white people haven't experienced the continuous harassment Black people have. A recent study has shown that this "paranoia" is healthy.[78]

Progress toward integration has been one-sided: Blacks have been integrated but not Whites; many Whites have not accepted integration. During the Reagan administration, the government started backtracking on enforcement.[79] Cases of female discrimination fare better than those of Black discrimination. In the case of *Faragher vs. the City of Boca Raton*, the Supreme Court decided that "although racial and sexual harassment will often take different forms, and standards may not be interchangeable, we think there is good sense in harmonizing the 'standards of actionable harassment.'" Blacks have few allies in the courts: Ruth Bader Ginsburg, John Paul Stevens, Stephen Gerald Breyer. Not Clarence Thomas, who should know better. And 1,816 out of 1,838 district attorneys are white. There is also evidence that in challenging jury selections, prosecutors make every effort to make the juries as white as possible.[80]

Recently there has been recognition of another form of discrimination: class discrimination against the lower class. With inequality growing, obstacles against advancement for the lower class has gotten worse. This could explain why the fortunes of less-skilled workers have declined, as well as the decline of aggregate productivity.[81]

Prejudice against African Americans went underground for a while. But prejudice against Hispanic Americans had always been in the open. Most undocumented workers are Hispanic. There is a legitimate concern regarding undocumented immigrants. We don't want criminals sneaking into our country, but the average undocumented immigrant just wants to work hard and improve his or her life. The statistical evidence shows that there are no more criminals among them than there are among the rest of the population. As a matter of fact, at the same time the undocumented immigrant population tripled, the crime rate dropped 18 percent annually.[82]

Some people have a problem with diversity. Their motive is not law enforcement but prejudice. These people are shooting themselves in the foot, because immigrants are consumers and, therefore, contribute to the economy, spending $1.5 trillion annually.

Americans should understand that prejudice is not only wrong, it undermines the economy. We need to fight against prejudice. But it does no good to preach. We need to understand those who are prejudiced. No, I'm not excusing prejudice. I'm saying we need to understand prejudice if we are going to deal with it. Some think they are losing status to minorities. They think there is too much attention paid to minorities and not enough to them. They fear they are losing their jobs to minorities.[83] In combating prejudice, continue to pay attention to minorities, but also pay attention to whites and convince them their legitimate complaints are largely the same as those of minorities.

Do you think undocumented immigrants are taking your job? Let me assure you, there's enough for all—if only the minimum wage were raised to a living standard. There's enough.

It's true that unlawful immigration costs the government money. Undocumented immigrants can't get welfare, but the government must spend extra money on education, parks, police, sewage, and other benefits for the extra population. And some undocumented immigrants have American-born children who, as US citizens have a right to welfare programs. In 2010, the average undocumented family received $24,721 in government benefits, paying only $10,334 in taxes, causing a deficit of $14,387.

But this is not just an undocumented-immigrant problem; it's also a US-citizen problem. In 2010, the average household headed by a US citizen without a high school diploma received $46,582 in government benefits, paying only $11,469 in taxes, generating a $35,113 deficit. Someone had to pay for these deficits.

In 2010, the average household headed by a citizen with a college degree received $24,839 in government benefits, paying $54,089, generating a surplus of $29,250.[84] The fault lies not with the immigrants but with the system.

The fault can very simply be corrected: raise the minimum wage to a living standard. Yes, undocumented immigrants are breaking the law, and they must be punished. And they are punished: their jobs are taken from them, their families are broken up, and they are handcuffed and imprisoned, all because of the lack of a piece of paper. Do you think they deserve this kind of punishment?

What about US lawbreakers? Sit on any Trax station long enough and you are bound to see several jaywalkers. Walk in any street and you will seldom see a motorist giving a pedestrian right-of-way at a crosswalk. Maybe you are one of them. The worst these lawbreakers get is a fine. If undocumented immigrants are ever threatened with deportation, they can have the protection of the habeas corpus law because that law applies to "persons," not "citizens." There is a precedent for this in the case of *Standing Bear v. Crook*.

In 1868, the federal government accidentally gave land belonging to the Ponca Indians to the Sioux. The federal government offered the Ponca Indians other land in American Indian territory. It turned out to be a forced relocation because the Poncas did not want to move. They were force-marched to other American Indian territory in inclement weather at the cost of many lives.

One of their chiefs, Standing Bear, walked away from American Indian territory with a small group and headed toward their homeland. They were caught and interned at Fort Omaha. Standing Bear got his case in court. His lawyers appealed to the habeas corpus law, and the judge couldn't find the word "citizen" anywhere in it. The words used were "person" and "party." Standing Bear was certainly a "person" who was a "party" in the case. So Judge Dundy, the presiding judge in the case, ruled that because Standing Bear had committed no crime and was not planning on committing a crime, he should be set free.

The case got a great deal of publicity, which got Standing Bear a lot of sympathy from the public.[85] So if any undocumented immigrants are threatened with deportation, they can appeal to the habeas corpus law. They can't be separated from their jobs, their families, or their freedoms. All they can get is a fine.

This will be a win for the US government also. It will make policing of the border much easier. Law-enforcement officials can concentrate on dealing with the real criminals. And the officials won't have to build a fence.

We wouldn't want to build a fence anyway. Mexicans are leaving because the Mexican economy is improving, reducing the number of undocumented immigrants from 12.2 million to 11.1 million. This is causing a shortage of labor! That's right—a shortage of labor. Many farms use undocumented immigrants to pick crops because native-born Americans don't want that job. Farms are already 50 percent short of labor, and if we lose too many more, we're in trouble. Farmers raise fewer crops, which would raise prices. Building trades have the same problem.[86]

I have said that ALEC supports companies that poison the environment. One of these corporations is the Canadian Oil Company, which damages the earth, sky, and water by mining tar sands. This is the company behind the Keystone Pipeline. I must point out that ALEC isn't the only one who wants tar sands oil, and not everyone who wants tar sands oil is an ALEC supporter. Fossil fuels were the energy that drove the Industrial Revolution. They were the most efficient source of energy, and in the beginning, it was not known what the environmental risks from using fossil fuels were. Industry became dependent on fossil fuels. When the effects of fossil fuels on the environment were discovered, scientists were concerned enough to experiment with renewable energy. This research was also motivated by a fear of running out of fossil fuels.

When tar sands oil was discovered, the fear of running out of oil ended. We now have a source that will last for the foreseeable future. There is now a strong temptation to rely on tar sands oil as a source of energy. Many people welcome this oil because it frees us from purchasing the foreign oil we import from troubled and unstable nations. What we really need, though, is to free ourselves from our dependence on fossil fuels. Our economy will not be sustainable indefinitely if we continue to depend on them.

The consequence will be an environmental crisis, sooner or later, and it will be worse than an economic crisis. Nature will not be forgiving. Science has the evidence, and ALEC simply denies the evidence of science. But scientific evidence should not be controversial. If we ignore scientific evidence, we are blindsighting ourselves.

What are tar sands? Tar sands are a mixture of sand, clay, water, and bitumen. Bitumen is a semisolid petroleum with the consistency of tar. The first step in mining tar sands is to get rid of the forest. The next step is to remove the topsoil and peat. Next, hot water is mixed with the tar sands to separate the bitumen from the other components. Chemicals are then added to get rid of any final traces of water, and the tar sand is then upgraded into a lighter consistency with enormous amounts of heat, pressure, and more chemicals. Finally, the tar sand is shipped to a refinery.

Some bitumen can be taken from the surface, but to get most of it, it is necessary to dig deeper.

Wells are dug, and steam is injected into the wells. This loosens the sand, and it is pumped through other wells. The sand, clay, and water are pumped into tailing ponds.[87] The process of mining tar sands is called "fracking." What's wrong with fracking? It destroys the natural environment. Forests are breeding grounds for migratory birds. Larger animals, such as deer, bears, and wolves, need a large amount of land on which to live. These tailing ponds, with all their poisonous chemicals, leech into ground and surface water. Processing the bitumen spreads poisonous particulates, such as nitrogen oxides, sulfur dioxide, and hydrogen sulfides, as well as large amounts of greenhouse gasses, into the air. Some of these particulates, such as polycyclic aromatic hydrocarbons, are carcinogenic.

Fracking also requires enormous amounts of water. It takes anywhere from two and a half to four barrels of water to extract one barrel of bitumen. It is difficult to recycle that amount of water for other uses.[88] Its extraction and refinement emits between 3.2 percent to 4.5 percent more carbon dioxide than conventional oil. Further, one gallon of tar sand bitumen emits between 14 percent to 37 percent more greenhouse gas than the same amount of conventional oil.[89]

And that's not all.

There are dollars-and-cents costs too. The cost of purifying contaminated drinking water is so expensive it is rarely done. For instance, Cabot Oil and Gas spent $109,000 to remove methane from well water for fourteen homes, and Colorado has spent eight years cleaning up underground seepage to the tune of thousands of dollars. Replacement of contaminated water is also expensive. Cabot Oil and Gas spent $193,000 in replacing water in homes with contaminated water. Fracking also pollutes the water in big-city water systems, increasing the cost of their filtration systems.

Businesses also pay the price of fracking in the form of employee absenteeism and lower production due to sickness from air pollution. The community also pays. Public health costs in the Fayetteville, Arkansas, shale region amounted to more than $10 million in 2008. In addition, fracking has hurt the $340 million hunting and wildlife-watching industry in Wyoming. The destruction of forest land has fragmented the wildlife habitat. Between 2001 and 2010, in one area the mule-deer population dropped 59 percent. Trucks carrying water to a single well create the equivalent in road damage of 3.5 million car trips. Texas has approved $400 million for road repair in the Barnett shale region, and Pennsylvania has estimated a cost of $265 million in the Marcellus shale region.

Another issue related to fracking is that thousands of orphaned gas wells have been left behind by the oil and gas industry. Cabot Oil and Gas spent $730,000 per well to cap three wells, but the public will probably foot the bill for capping most of them. The value of houses is also decreased by fracking. Houses worth $250,000 that are within one thousand feet of a well have their value decreased by 3 to 14 percent. Farms are hurt by fracking through exposure of livestock to wastewater spills and the difficulty of getting water for farming. In the Pennsylvania Marcellus fracking area, there was an 18.5 percent reduction in milk production.[90]

And there are social costs as well. The mines create boom towns that attract all kinds of people who bring crime with them. For example, in the middle of Montana's and North Dakota's tar sands boom, the town of Watford, North Dakota, saw a 565 percent increase in arrests since 2005. Roosevelt County in Montana saw an 855 percent increase in arrests during the same time period.[91]

So, what, you ask, does this have to do with the consumer? The consumer will have to pay the consequences of fracking. The consumer will have to pay large sums of money—money that otherwise could be spent on other things—to adapt to the new environment. Businesses will have to do the same, which will mean higher prices for the consumer. Government will also have to do the same, which will again mean higher taxes for the consumer. And ALEC will have to pay along with everyone else. We may already be paying the price.

In the past fifty years, the temperature has risen at a faster rate than at any time during recorded history. All but one of the sixteen hottest recorded temperatures happened after 2000.[92] Extreme heatwaves have caused hundreds of deaths from heat exhaustion, and cardiovascular and kidney diseases. Rising temperatures increase ground-level ozone, a component of smog and dirty air that is bad for asthma, hay fever, and allergies.[93] In 2015 alone, there were as many as ten natural disasters of all types—storms, droughts, floods, wild fires[94]—all fueled by rising temperatures. The California drought saw the worst water shortage in twelve hundred years, ramped up to 15 to 20 percent by the heat. The rise of ocean temperatures increases the energy in hurricanes—from category three to category four, the frequency of hurricanes having increased since the 1980s.[95]

An illustrative case is Hurricane Sandy, which devastated the East Coast in the summer of 2012. It is thought that Sandy was the result of climate change. It caused $68 billion worth of damage to 650,000 homes and claimed 181 lives. One year later, the victims still had not received most of the $60 billion in federal aid they were promised. This may be a preview of things to come. The National Oceanic and Atmospheric Administration says that rising temperatures increase the chance of another superstorm hitting New York City by 50 percent. *The Week* magazine asks whether Americans are prepared to pay $60 billion every five or ten years to rebuild after every storm. The only alternative would be for everyone to move out of coastal areas where the storms would occur. That would be expensive enough. Approximately 123 million Americans, more than one-third of the entire population, live in those areas, and approximately 1.7 million of them live only a few feet from the ocean at high tide. With rising sea levels, these people would have no other option but to move out.[96]

According to a United Nations panel of leading environmental scientists, millions could be displaced by floods and drought. Food supplies could be endangered. Wars could be fought over dwindling resources. The chairman of the panel, Rajendra Pachauri, says that "nobody on this planet is going to be untouched by climate change."[97]

In 2015, President Obama was an environmental leader in a conference on climate change. The participants hoped to reverse climate change by reducing greenhouse-gas emissions. The goal of the conference was to decrease pollution to keep the temperature from rising more than 1.5° C above preindustrial levels. The nations were to meet every five years after 2020. After 2023, they were to report regularly on their progress. Obama pledged $3 billion to the Green Climate Fund, an organization that assists third-world nations in adopting cleaner air technologies.[98]

Who are the global-warming deniers? First of all, there are the fossil-fuel industries—oil and coal. Of course. Who else? They say they can prove global warming is a hoax. Jim Inhofe, chairman of the Senate Committee on Environmental and Public Works, and also an oil lobbyist, said that climate change "is the greatest hoax ever perpetrated on the American people." He brought a snowball into the Senate chamber and threw it across the floor in order, he said, "to refute the hoax."[99]

This refutation is highly organized. It is called a "denial machine." It is supported by the fossil fuels lobby, the Koch Brothers, industry advocates, Libertarian think tanks and the "conservative" media. It has found a model in the campaign of tobacco companies to "prove" tobacco is harmless by manufacturing scientific sounding disinformation. In other words, they are lying. Their scientists have done the research and gotten the answers. But the answers they have given the public are based on fake science—

the same trick the tobacco companies pulled on the public to fool them into thinking tobacco was safe. But they are convincing those who have strongly held beliefs that don't jibe with climate change.[100]

Who are these people? Dr. Randal K. Olsen, senior data scientist of the University of Pennsylvania, has done some research on the subject. He finds that, surprisingly, income and education have nothing to do with it. He found that two groups tend to be global-warming deniers: conservatives and religious people.[101] Keep in mind, this is a statistical study. There are exceptions. Why are conservatives global-warming deniers? They fear that environmental measures obstruct free enterprise. They want to protect free enterprise. Environmentalists want to protect the environment. One can do both.[102] Steven M. Meyer, a professor at the Massachusetts Institute of Technology, did an investigation titled "Environmentalism and Economic Prosperity." He examined several cities, some with strong environmental policies, others with weak ones. He used five economic indicators. He found that four of the five indicators tested positive for cities with strong environmental policy, but not those with weak ones. Cautiously, he conceded that other factors might be involved. But in any case, the research showed that environmentalism does not impact economic prosperity.

IRENA, an intergovernmental agency that promotes renewable energy, found that renewable energy would increase gross national product by 0.6 to 1.1 percent. It would create 24 million jobs, mostly in biotechnology, hydropower, and solar energy.

Why are religious people global-warming deniers? Many of them have a problem with science because it contradicts some of their beliefs. But environmentalism itself is completely congruent with religion and ought to be an integral part it. Christians are commanded to multiply and replenish the earth. What does "replenish the earth" mean? It is not a synonym for "multiply." It means "Take care of the earth, restore it after use." That is exactly what conservation is.

My advice to environmentalists: Forget about melting glaciers and rising sea levels. They're too remote from everyday experience. And don't think saying "Science says" will be more convincing. Focus on the consumer's pocket book. If they worry about that, they will worry about the other things without prompting.

ALEC operates private prisons, a profit-making enterprise at the taxpayer's expense. The private prison industry began with the inception of the war on drugs begun under the Nixon administration and has been waged by every president since. This was also a time when the public was concerned about crime, and candidates promised their constituents that they would be "tough on crime." Hundreds of drug users who should have been given therapy were jailed, and felons were given mandatory sentences. Prisons were running out of space, and some businessmen saw an opportunity.[103] A cofounder of the industry said that his company was founded on the principle that you could sell prisons "just like you were selling cars, or real estate, or hamburgers."[104]

As a result, the United States imprisons more people than any other nation. The next highest is Rwanda, followed by Russia and Cuba.[105] America's prison population is now 2.4 million, at a cost of $80 billion a year.[106] Of this 2.4 million, 6 percent of state prisoners and 16 percent of federal prisoners are in private prisons.[107] Most of them have committed low-level, nonviolent crimes, like drug or property offenses.[108] Undocumented immigrants are a major source of prisoners for private prisons. Families are broken up, and men, women, and children are imprisoned for up to ten months or longer. Immigration reform will eliminate this source. The private prison CEOs don't want this to happen.

If a reform bill is passed, private prison CEOs want the severe penalties that currently exist to be preserved in the bill. "Operation Streamline" was begun in 2005 to lobby for this.[109] Private prison CEOs claim that private prisons save the government money. This is nonsense, and it should be obvious. They are not selling anything. Where do they get the profits? The only possible source is the government (i.e., the taxpayer). And they are making a profit!

The two largest prison companies, Corrections Corporation of America and the Geo Group, received $3 billion, and top executives took home compensation packages of over $3 million.[110] Private prisons offer alternative careers for public sector bureaucrats looking to increase their income, including the FBI. Lawmakers also make money from private prisons. A former Tennessee governor Lamar Alexander and his wife, Honey, owned stock in Corporation of America. Manny Aragon, a New Mexico legislator, was also hired by Wackenhut to lobby for establishing private prisons in his state.[111]

Private prisons contract their prisoners as labor to corporations including Starbucks, McDonald's, Victoria's Secret, Boeing, and the military. These prisoners get paid anywhere from ninety-three cents to four dollars, but they don't receive benefits. Republican Representative Bill Huizenga of Michigan says, "This is not only a threat to established industries, it's also a threat to emerging industries."[112] How efficiently are private prisons run? They maximize profits by minimizing staff, including security, as well as services such as food, clothing, and medical. They are not held to the same standard as public prisons because they are private property.[113]

ALEC is waging war on the consumer on several fronts, including war on the people it depends on for its profits. ALEC is raping Mother Earth, on whom it is also dependent. What in the name of reason is ALEC thinking?! The members of ALEC are not evil, they are sick. They are addicted to money. Money to them is like candy to a child. They will do anything to get their hands on it. They lie, cheat, and steal to get it, and they don't think of the consequences. They can't wait; they want it now. And they want all of it. This is the mindset of a six-year-old.

But still, people vote for ALEC. ALEC appeals to the six-year-old in all of us. ALEC peddles freedom without responsibility. It promises irresponsible tax cuts and opposes necessary regulation. No one likes to pay taxes.

No one likes to be regulated. But if we wish to fight the demons of greed, ignorance, and indifference, we must first confront our own inner demons.

The members of ALEC are easily confused with those who have honest reasons for opposing high taxes and burdensome regulations. The conservatives who fought and won the American and French Revolutions and who fought against the tyranny of King George III and King Louis XIV won freedom for us all. They still see the faces of King George and King Louis in government.

Then there are others, equally honest liberals, who note that King George and King Louis are gone and that government is in the hands of the people and should have the power to serve the people. Republicans are conservative, Democrats are liberal.

How can we tell the difference between ALEC and its peers? The latter are reasonable. ALEC causes gridlock, and it threatens to close down the government if it doesn't get its way. Get the members of ALEC out of Congress and we will get our government back. There is nothing wrong with Congress, but it only works with reasonable people.

The members of ALEC call themselves conservatives. Is the boss paying his workers starvation wages conservative? Is polluting the environment conservative? Is shutting down the government conservative? What do the members of ALEC know about Conservatism? They don't have a clue. Who are the real conservatives? They are the conservationists— not only those who conserve our natural resources, but also those who conserve our human resources, the consumers. There is an intimate connection between natural and human conservation.

I have tried to prove that "it is better to give than to receive." Does this phrase sound familiar? It is a quotation of Jesus. I have also tried to prove that "the love of money is the root of all evil." St. Paul said that.

No, I'm not preaching religion. But I think that Jesus and St. Paul deserve the Nobel Prize for economics. I might add, "One cannot worship both God and Mammon." Jesus also said that. In secular terms, these sayings mean that ALEC is neither conservative, nor liberal, nor honest.

We need to care about each other because we are dependent on each other. This is not just a moral precept; it is an economic fact. The worker depends on their boss for their job. The boss depends on his or her workers to get their work done. The consumer depends on the boss and the boss's workers for the products and services the consumer needs. The boss and the workers depend on the consumers for their profits and wages. So, when you think of people in poverty, don't think, "That's too bad, but it's not my problem." It is your problem. It's my problem. It's everyone's problem because poverty is a sinkhole down which the entire economy is sliding. The only way we can plug the hole is for everyone to earn a living wage. There is no other way.

Bibliography

"A Case for the Minimum Wage of $15." *The Week*, July 5–12, 2013.

"A Kinder, Smarter Capitalism." *The Week*, September 14, 2012.

Allen, Christopher S. "Codetermination." Edited by Joel Krieger. *Politics of the World*, n.d., 149.

"A Recovery Felt by Few Americans." *The Week*, October 2, 2015.

"A Sea Change in American Spending." *The Week*, July 5–12.

"A Sea Change in American Spending." *The Week*, June 28, 2013.

"A Sea Change in American Spending." *The Week*, June 7, 2013.

Blyth, Mark. "The Austerity Delusion: Why a Bad Idea Won Over the West." *Foreign Affairs*. May/June 2013, 41.

"Bridge Collapses: More to Come?" *The Week*, June 7, 2013.

"Cars Can Fuel the Recovery." *The Week*, July 5–12, 2013.

"CBO Says Wage Hikes Could Cost Jobs." *The Week*, February 28, 2013.

"Climate Report Offers a Grim Forecast." *The Week*, April 11, 2014.

"Cruz vs. McCain." *The Week*, June 7, 2013.

Davis, Richard. "Minimum Wage Increase Is a Question of Fairness." *Deseret News*, September 4, 2013.

"Debt-Ridden Detroit Files Bankruptcy." *The Week*, August 2, 2013.

Dionne, E. J. "The Deficit Is Still the Wrong Problem." *Washington Post*, October 28, 2013.

"Fast Food Workers: Do They Deserve a Living Wage?" *The Week*, August 16–23, 2013.

Harvey, David. *The Enigma of Capital: And the Crises of Capitalism*. New York: Oxford University Press, 2010.

"Home Prices and Confidence Rise." *The Week*, June 07, 2013.

"House Speaker: The Open Warfare within the GOP." *The Week*, October 23, 2015.

http://wwwacku.org/prisoners-right/banking-prisons-and-mass-incarceration.

"Hurricane Sandy: The Misery Goes On." *The Week*, November 8, 2013.

Ibid., March 28, 2014, Noted, p. 34.

Ibid., November, 20, 2015, Noted, p. 16.

"Inequality; Is the American Dream Dying?" *The Week*, December 13, 2013.

Internet, Agenda.

Internet, ALEC Exposed.

Internet, ALEC.

Internet, Social Security

Internet. Tar Sands: Part of the Solution, or Part of the Problem?"

Internet. Undocumented Immigrants.

"Issue of the Week: Should the Minimum Wage Be Increased?" *The Week*, December 13, 2013.

"Issue of the Week: What Does Black Friday Tell Us?" *The Week*, December 13, 2013.

Johnston, David Cay. *Perfectly Legal: The Covert Campaign to Rig Our Tax System to Benefit the Super Rich—and Cheat Everybody Else.* n.p.: Portfolio, 2005.

Krugman, Paul. "Our Economic Problems Are Here and Now." *Salt Lake Tribune*, June 18, 2013.

Lynch, Robert G. *Do State & Local Tax Incentives Work?* Washington, D.C.: Economic Policy Institute, 1996.

"Our Country's True Job Creators." December 8, 2011. http://theweek.com/articles/479592/countrys-true-job-creators.

"Our Two Legal Systems." *The Week*, March 29, 2013.

"Private Sector Adds 135,000 Jobs." *The Week*, June 14, 2013.

"Rethinking Mandatory Sentencing." *The Week*, September 20, 2013.

Samuelson, Robert J. "Between Labor and Capital, Workers Are Losing." *Deseret News*, September 10, 2013.

Shilling, A. Gary. "V. Is for Vicious Circle." *Forbes*, August 30, 2009.

Stein, Mark. *How the States Got Their Shapes Too: The People Behind the Borderlines*. Washington: Smithsonian Institution Press, 2012.

Stockman, Lorne, David Turnbull, and Stephen Kretzmann. *Petroleum Coke: The Coal Hiding in the Tar Sands*. n.p.: Oil Change International, 2013. http://priceofoil.org/content/uploads/2013/01/OCI.Petcoke.FINALSCREEN.pdf.

Striner, Richard. *Lincoln's Way: How Six Great Presidents Created American Power*, Rowman & Littlefield, 2010.

"Tax Cuts Don't Produce Growth." *The Week*, September 28, 2012.

"The Bottom Line." *The Week*, July 5–12.

"The Bottom Line." *The Week*, June 7, 2013.

"The Economy's New Normal." *The Week*, November 28, 2013.

"The GOPs Sobering Self-Diagnosis." *The Week*, March 29, 2013.

"The Minimum Wage: Should It Be Raised?" *The Week*, December 13, 2013.

"The War on Poverty: Success or Failure?" *The Week*, January 24, 2014.

The Week, Dec. 13, 2013, Noted, 16.

The Week, June 28, 2013, Noted, 13.

"Why Taxes Must Go Up, Not Down." *The Week*, November 12, 2015.

"Working, But Still Poor." *The Week*, February 08, 2013.

"World Must Adapt to Climate Change." *The Week*, November 20, 2015.

www.mintpressnews.com.

wwwepi.org/unions/Utah/44.

Notes

1 "Our Country's True Job Creators," *The Week*, December 8, 2011, http://theweek.com/articles/479592/countrys-true-job-creators.

2 A. Gary Shilling, "V. Is for Vicious Circle," *Forbes*, August 30, 2009, 126.

3 "Working, But Still Poor," *The Week*, February 8, 2013, 11.

4 David Harvey, *The Enigma of Capital: And the Crises of Capitalism* (New York: Oxford University Press, 2010), 1–2.

5 "Home Prices and Confidence Rise," *The Week*, June 7, 2013, 35.

6 "Cars Can fuel the recovery," *The Week*, July 5–12, 2013, 38.

7 "The Bottom Line," *The Week*, June 7, 2013, 35.

8 "Private Sector Adds 135,000 Jobs," *The Week*, June 14, 2013, 35.

9 "A Sea Change in American Spending," *The Week*, June 28, 2013, 34.

10 Ibid., 34.

11 "Noted," *The Week*, June 7, 2013, 18.

12 "The Bottom Line," *The Week*, July 5–12, 36.

13 "Noted," 18.

14 "A Sea Change in American Spending," *The Week*, July 5–12, 34.

[15] "Special Report: Automation Puts Jobs in Peril."

[16] Ibid.

[17] "Special report: Automation Puts Jobs in Peril."

[18] "Debt-Ridden Detroit Files Bankruptcy," *The Week*, August 2, 2013, 2.

[19] "Ten Tax Payer Handouts to The Super Rich That Will Make Your Blood Boil."

[20] "A Recovery Felt by Few Americans," *The Week*, October 2, 2015.

[21] "Great White Hopes," *New Republic*, Jan./Feb. 2017, 16.

[22] "Tax Cuts Don't Produce Growth," *The Week*, September 28, 2012.

[23] Mark Blyth, "The Austerity Delusion: Why a Bad Idea Won Over the West," *Foreign Affairs*, May/June 2013.

[24] "Decaying Infrastructure Cost U.S. Billions Each Year," report says.

[25] Ibid.

[26] "Bridge Collapses: More to Come?" *The Week*, June 7, 2013, 19.

[27] "Our Two Legal Systems," *The Week*, March 29, 2013.

[28] E. J. Dionne, "The Deficit Is Still the Wrong Problem," *Washington Post*, October 28, 2013.

[29] Paul Krugman, "Our Economic Problems Are Here and Now," *Salt Lake Tribune*, June 18, 2013.

[30] For an interesting discussion on this issue, see Richard Striner, *Lincoln's Way: How Six Great Presidents Created American Power*, Rowman & Littlefield, 2010.

[31] "The Economy's New Normal," *The Week*, November 28, 2013.

[32] Richard Davis, "Minimum Wage Increase Is a Question of Fairness," *Deseret News*, September 04, 2013, A11.

[33] "A Kinder, Smarter Capitalism," *The Week*, September 14, 2012.

[34] Robert J. Samuelson, "Between Labor and Capital, Workers Are Losing," *Deseret News*, September 10, 2013, A11.

[35] Davis, op. cit., A11.

[36] Samuelson, op. cit., A11.

[37] "Issue of the Week: What Does Black Friday Tell Us?" *The Week*, December 13, 2013.

[38] "Inequality: Is the American Dream Dying?" *The Week*, December 13, 2013.

[39] "Issue of the Week: Should the Minimum Wage Be Increased?" *The Week*, December 13, 2013.

[40] "Fast Food Workers: Do They Deserve a Living Wage?" *The Week*, August 16–23, 2013.

[41] "The Minimum Wage: Should It Be Raised?" *The Week*, December 13, 2013.

[42] Samuelson, op cit., A11.

[43] "A Case for the Minimum Wage of $15," *The Week*, July 5–12, 2013.

[44] "CBO Says Wage Hikes Could Cost Jobs," *The Week*, February 28, 2013.

[45] Internet, ALEC.

[46] "Decaying Infrastructure Costs U.S. Billions Each Year, Report Says."

[47] "The Relentless Pace of Automation"—technologyreview.com.

[48] "The Relentless Pace of Automation."

[49] "The Relentless Pace of Automation."

[50] "Advantages and Disadvantages of Driverless Cars."

[51] "Rescuing the Rust Belt," *The Week*, March 24, 2017, 11.

[52] "The Bottom Line," *The Week*, March 31, 2017, 13.

[53] "Top 10 NASA Inventions We Use Every Day."

[54] Richard A. Muller, "Now: The Physics of Time," W. W. Norton & Co., 2016, 146.

[55] Internet, American Legislative Exchange Council-Source Watch.

[56] Internet, "Who is ALEC?—ALEC Exposed."

[57] Internet, Internet American Legislative Exchange Council-Source Watch.

[58] *The Week*, June 28, 2013, Noted, 13.

[59] "The GOP'S Sobering Self-Diagnosis," *The Week*, March 29, 2013.

[60] "Cruz vs. McCain," *The Week*, June 7, 2013.

[61] "House Speaker: The Open Warfare within the GOP," *The Week*, October 23, 2015.

[62] www.epi.org/unions/Utah/44

[63] Christopher S. Allen, "Codetermination," ed. Joel Krieger, *Politics of the World.*

[64] "NAFTA Legacy: Who Won, Who Lost," *The Week*, February 24, 2017, 11.

[65] Issue of the week: Businesses Battle over Border Tax," *The Week*, April 14, 2017, 38.

[66] "Ten Tax Payer Handouts to The Super Rich That Will Make Your Blood Boil."

[67] Robert G. Lynch, Do State & Local Tax Incentives Work? (Washington, D.C.: Economic Policy Institute, 1996). Passim.

[68] Ibid., 23.

[69] "Ten Tax Payer Handouts to The Super Rich That Will Make Your Blood Boil."

[70] David Cay Johnston, *Perfectly Legal: The Covert Campaign to Rig Our Tax System to Benefit the Super Rich—and Cheat Everybody Else* (n.p.: Portfolio, 2005), 23.

[71] Ibid., 5.

[72] "The War on Poverty: Success or Failure?" *The Week*, January 24, 2014.

[73] Internet, "Social Security's Impact on the Economy," *The Huffington Post.*

[74] "Why Taxes Must Go Up, Not Down," *The Week*, November 12, 2015, 12.

[75] "Discrimination Doesn't Make Dollars, or Sense."

[76] "The Cost of Discrimination in the Workplace."

[77] "The Many Costs of Discrimination: The Case of Middle-Class African Americans."

[78] Ibid.

[79] "Discrimination Doesn't Make Dollars, or Sense."

[80] "The Many Costs of Discrimination: The Case of Middle-Class African Americans."

[81] "Discrimination Doesn't Make Dollars, or Sense."

[82] "Rockville Rape: Fueling the Immigration Debate," *The Week*, April 7, 2017, 17.

[83] "Great White Hopes," *New Republic*, January/February, 16.

[84] Robert Rector and Jason Richwine, "The Fiscal Cost of Unlawful Immigrants and Amnesty to the U.S. Taxpayer," The Heritage Foundation, May 06, 2013, http://www.heritage.org/research/reports/2013/05/the-fiscal-cost-of-unlawful-immigrants-and-amnesty-to-the-us-taxpayer.

[85] Mark Stein, *How the States Got Their Shapes Too: The People Behind the Borderlines* (Washington: Smithsonian Institution Press, 2012), 261–71.

[86] "We Deport Immigrants at Our Peril," *The Week*, March 10, 2017, 4.

[87] Internet, "Carbon Capture and Storage: Part of the Solution, or Part of the Problem?"

[88] Ibid.

[89] Lorne Stockman, David Turnbull, and Stephen Kretzmann, *Petroleum Coke: The Coal Hiding in the*

Tar Sands (n.p.: Oil Change International, 2013), http://priceofoil.org/content/uploads/2013/01/OCI. Petcoke
.FINALSCREEN.pdf.

[90] Internet, "The Costs of Fracking."

[91] *The Week*, December 13, 2013, Noted, 16.

[92] "Global Warming: Facts, Definitions, Causes and Effects."

[93] "Related Stories: Are the Effects of Global Warming All That Bad?"

[94] Op. cit., "Related Stories" Ibid.

[95] "Global Warming: Facts, Definitions, Causes and Effects."

[96] "Hurricane Sandy: The Misery Goes On," *The Week*, November 8, 2013.

[97] "Climate Report Offers a Grim Forecast," *The Week*, April 11, 2014.

[98] "Global Warming: Facts, Definitions, Causes and Effects."

[99] "Climate Change Denial," Wikipedia.

[100] Ibid.

[101] Dr. Randal K. Olson, "Who Are the Climate Change Deniers?"

[102] "Why Conservatives Deny Climate Change."

[103] Matt Stroud, "'Just Like Selling Hamburgers': 30 Years of Private Prisons in the U.S.," *Forbes*, June 21, 2013, http://www.forbes.com/sites/matt-

stroud/2013/06/21/just-like-selling-hamburgers-30-years-of-private-prisons-in-the-u-s/#6fb3c9eb49f2.

[104] www.mintpressnews.com.

[105] "Rethinking Mandatory Sentencing," *The Week*, September 20, 2013.

[106] http://wwwacku.org/prisoners-right/banking-prisons-and-mass-incarceration.

[107] www.mintpressnews.com.

[108] http:/huffingtonpost.com/laura-carleson/immigration-private-prison-Lobby-b2665188html.

[109] http:/huffingtonpost.com/laura-carleson/immigration-private-prison-Lobby-b2665188html.

[110] Ibid.

[111]   http://correctoinsprospect.com/corrections/prishtm-23k.

[112]   http://finance.yahoo.com/blogs/daily-ticker/top-5-secrets-private-prisnpundustry.

[113] Internet, "For profit prisons: eight statistics that show the problems."

About the Author

Leon Johnson is a retired janitor. A self-made intellect who reads a lot, he thinks everyone should do the same. He is a history buff and a science buff who has spent much of his life volunteering in politics and community affairs. He has been awarded the Democratic Taylor-Mayne Award for Outstanding Service. *Who's the Goose that Lays the Golden Egg?* is a fresh new look at the complicated economic problems facing Americans today. He hopes it will encourage people to think outside the box as they look for positive solutions. He currently lives in West Valley City, Utah.

stroud/2013/06/21/just-like-selling-hamburgers-30-
years-of-private-prisons-in-the-u-s/#6fb3c9eb49f2.
[104] www.mintpressnews.com.
[105] "Rethinking Mandatory Sentencing," *The Week*,
September 20, 2013.
[106] http://wwwacku.org/prisoners-right/banking-pris-
ons-and-mass-incarceration.
[107] www.mintpressnews.com.
[108] http:/huffingtonpost.com/laura-carleson/immigra-
tion-private-prison-Lobby-b2665188html.
[109] http:/huffingtonpost.com/laura-carleson/immigra-
tion-private-prison-Lobby-b2665188html.
[110] Ibid.
[111]   http://correctoinsprospect.com/corrections/pr-
ishtm-23k.
[112]   http://finance.yahoo.com/blogs/daily-ticker/
top-5-secrets-private-prisnpundustry.
[113] Internet, "For profit prisons: eight statistics that
show the problems."

About the Author

Leon Johnson is a retired janitor. A self-made intellect who reads a lot, he thinks everyone should do the same. He is a history buff and a science buff who has spent much of his life volunteering in politics and community affairs. He has been awarded the Democratic Taylor-Mayne Award for Outstanding Service. *Who's the Goose that Lays the Golden Egg?* is a fresh new look at the complicated economic problems facing Americans today. He hopes it will encourage people to think outside the box as they look for positive solutions. He currently lives in West Valley City, Utah.